Count Your Way through
Greece

by Jim Haskins and Kathleen Benson

illustrations by Janice Lee Porter

Carolrhoda Books, Inc. / Minneapolis

To Margaret Emily

This book is available in two editions:
Library binding by Carolrhoda Books, Inc.,
   a division of Lerner Publishing Group
Soft cover by First Avenue Editions,
   an imprint of Lerner Publishing Group
241 First Avenue North
Minneapolis, MN 55401 U.S.A.

Website address: www.lernerbooks.com

Library of Congress Cataloging-in-Publication Data

Haskins, James.
   Count your way through Greece / by Jim Haskins and Kathleen Benson ; illustrated by Janice Lee Porter.
      p.   cm.
   ISBN 0-87614-875-5 (lib. bdg. : alk. paper)
   ISBN 0-87614-973-5 (pbk. : alk. paper)
   1. Greece—Civilization—Juvenile literature. 2. Greek language, Modern—Numerals—Juvenile literature. 3. Counting—Juvenile literature. I. Benson, Kathleen. II. Porter, Janice Lee. III. Title.
DF741.H36 1996
949.5—dc20   95-39348

Manufactured in the United States of America
3 4 5 6 7 8 – JR – 05 04 03 02 01 00

Introductory Note

The Greek alphabet was developed around 1000 B.C. It is the direct or indirect ancestor of all modern European alphabets. Although the letters may look strange to Americans, the Greek alphabet is closely related to the alphabet we use to write American English.

The English language has borrowed many words from the Greek, including *music* and *astronaut.* The English word *alphabet* comes from the Greek names for the letters *a (alpha)* and *b (beta).*

In ancient times, Greek power and influence spread across Europe and Asia. Ancient Greek culture has given us more than just our language. It is also an ancestor of our system of government. And we continue to study and appreciate ancient Greek literature, architecture, and sculpture.

1 ένα (EH-nah)

Greece has **one** official religion. More than 95 percent of the people of Greece are members of the Greek Orthodox Church. Greek Orthodoxy is a form of Christianity that is similar to Catholicism. Although the government of Greece recognizes Greek Orthodoxy as the country's official church, the people can choose any religion they like. Other Western nations, such as the United States, keep church and government separate.

Religion is very important to most Greek people. In many towns and villages, very little is done without the blessing of the local priest. Religious festivals, especially those held at Easter, are the most important celebrations of the year.

2 δύο (THEE-oh)

Two main occupations of the people who live on Greece's many islands are fishing and harvesting sponges.

Fishing has long been important to the Greek economy. The waters surrounding Greece hold mullet, tuna, sardines, and many other species of fish. The Greek people eat some of the fish they catch and export the rest. Unfortunately, overfishing and pollution have reduced the numbers of fish and made it more difficult for Greek islanders to make a living at fishing.

Sponges have become a more important export than fish in Greece. These marine animals attach themselves to rocks and coral beneath the sea. In deep water, the islanders dive for sponges. In shallow water, they rake sponges up with long-handled forks. People use the dried skeletons of sponges, which are soft and very absorbent, for cleaning and bathing.

3 τρία **(TREE-ah)**

Three traditional crafts still practiced in Greece are embroidery, metalwork, and pottery making. Visitors to Greece seek out colorful embroidered tablecloths, handkerchiefs, and clothing. They also buy traditional jewelry made by skilled Greek metalworkers, and beautiful hand-painted pots. Many examples of ancient Greek pottery can be found in museums around the world. The scenes on the pots can tell us a great deal about life in ancient Greece.

4 τέσσερα (TEH-seh-rah)

The ancient Greeks were pioneers in **four** areas: medicine, biology, physics, and mathematics.

The Greek physician Hippocrates (hih-PAH-kruh-teez) is considered to be the father of medicine. He insisted that disease was not a punishment from the gods but a result of the way people lived. He believed that doctors had certain responsibilities, which he described in what came to be known as the Hippocratic oath.

The ancient Greeks advanced what people knew about biology by studying animals. The Greek philosopher Aristotle (ar-uh-STAH-tehl) was the first to classify animals into different groups.

If you study physics, you will learn that everything is made up of tiny pieces of matter called atoms. This idea was first suggested by Greek philosopher Leucippus (loo-KIH-puhs) in the 400s B.C. Ancient Greeks Pythagoras (puh-THA-guh-ruhs) and Euclid (YOO-klehd) made contributions to mathematics that we still use.

WATER·EARTH·FIRE·AIR

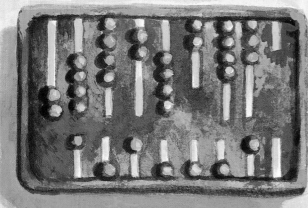

ΑΣΚΛΗ
ΠΙΩ
ΚΑΙ
ΥΓΕΙΑ
ΤΥΧΗ

ΕΥΧΑΡΙΣ
ΤΗΡΙΟΝ

5 πέντε (PEHN-teh)

The symbol for the Olympic Games, which began in Greece about 3,000 years ago, is **five** intertwined rings. The rings stand for the five continents that are home to the athletes who compete in the Olympics: Africa, Asia, Australia, Europe, and North and South America, which are counted as one.

There are many legends about the start of the Olympics. The first recorded Olympic competition was a footrace held in the Greek city of Olympia in 776 B.C. Later, such events as the discus throw, the javelin throw, the long jump, boxing, and wrestling were added. The games, which were held every four years, came to symbolize peace and fair play. The last of the ancient Olympics was held in A.D. 388.

The Olympic Games were revived more than 1,500 years later by Frenchman Pierre de Coubertin. The first modern Olympics were held in Athens, the capital of Greece, in 1896. With a few interruptions because of war, the games have been held every four years since then in various cities of the world.

6 ἕξι (EX-ee)

The ancient Greeks worshipped many gods and goddesses. They believed that the **six** most important gods and goddesses ruled from Mount Olympus.

The six gods were:
Zeus (ZOOS)—ruler of the gods
Apollo (uh-PAH-loh)—god of music, poetry, and purity. Twin brother of Artemis
Ares (AR-eez)—god of war
Hephaestus (hee-FEH-stuhs)—blacksmith for the gods
Poseidon (poh-SY-duhn)—god of the ocean and earthquakes
Hermes (HUHR-meez)—messenger for the gods

The six goddesses were:
Hera (HEE-ruh)—sister and wife of Zeus
Athena (uh-THEE-nuh)—goddess of wisdom and war
Aphrodite (af-ruh-DY-tee)—goddess of love
Artemis (AHR-tuh-mihs)—goddess of hunting. Twin sister of Apollo
Demeter (dih-MEE-tuhr)—goddess of agriculture
Hestia (HEH-stee-uh)—goddess of the hearth

HEPHAESTUS   HESTIA

The ancient Greeks built temples and other monuments to honor these gods and goddesses. Their stories can be read today as Greek mythology.

ZEUS HERA

APHRODITE HERMES

ARES

ATHENA

ARTEMIS

APOLLO

POSEIDON DEMETER

7 εφτά (ehf-TAH)

Seven ingredients often used in Greek cooking are lemons, olives and olive oil, yogurt, lamb, eggplant, honey, and grape leaves.

Souvlakia (soov-LAH-kee-uh) is a traditional Greek dish that features cubes of lamb coated in olive oil and lemon juice and cooked on skewers. Moussaka (moo-suh-KAH) is a dish made up of layers of eggplant, minced meat, potato, and onion. Dolmades (dohl-MAH-theez) are grape leaves stuffed with various foods, usually rice and herbs. Baklava (bah-kluh-VAH) is a rich dessert made of thin layers of buttery pastry, nuts, and honey.

8 οχτώ (ohk-TOH)

There are **eight** columns at each end of the Parthenon (PAHR-thuh-nahn), a magnificent marble temple in the Greek city of Athens. The Parthenon was built in the 400s B.C. to honor the goddess Athena. It stands on a hill called the Acropolis (uh-KRAH-puh-luhs), which means "high place." Although the temple has been damaged over time, it is still the most striking of all the ruins of ancient monuments and buildings on the Acropolis.

 **εννιά (eh-nee-AH)**

There are **nine** stripes on the Greek flag, five blue and four white. There is one stripe for each of the country's nine regions: Thrace, Macedonia (ma-suh-DOH-nee-uh), Thessaly, Epirus (ih-PY-ruhs), Central Greece and Euboea (yuh-BEE-eh), the Peloponnesus (peh-luh-puh-NEE-suhs), the Ionian Islands, the Aegean (ih-JEE-uhn) Islands, and Crete.

The color blue stands for the sea and the sky. The color white represents the Greek struggle for independence. The white cross in the corner of the flag refers to the state religion, Greek Orthodoxy.

10 δέκα (THEH-kah)

Ten animals featured in the fables of Greek storyteller Aesop (EE-sahp) are a dog, camel, grasshopper, pig, stork, tortoise, fox, ant, hare, and monkey.

Aesop lived on the Greek island of Samos. His fables seem to be about animals, but each story contains a message, or moral, for people. "The Tortoise and the Hare" is probably Aesop's most famous fable. This story is about a race between a slow-moving tortoise and a speedy hare. The well-known moral of the story is "slow and steady wins the race."

Pronunciation Guide

1 / ένα / EH-nah

2 / δύο / THEE-oh

3 / τρία / TREE-ah

4 / τέσσερα / TEH-seh-rah

5 / πέντε / PEHN-teh

6 / έζι / EX-ee

7 / εφτά / ehf-TAH

8 / οχτώ / ohk-TOH

9 / εννιά / eh-nee-AH

10 / δέκα / THEH-kah